Praise for BOSS CUPID

"Self-consciously 'dancing in chains,' in Nietzsche's phrase, Gunn allows his patterns of meter, rhyme and stanzaic form to emerge organically from the material to which he is seeking to give shape. One can almost follow this happening on the page, observation finding its proper rhythm, emotion its spiritual level, the poet discovering new moods, new modes of reflection." —WILLIAM DERESIEWICZ
The New York Times Book Review

"The tone of sadness Gunn strikes so repeatedly and so well is always mixed with something else, and it's the combination that makes the poetry human and distinct. I feel, reading Thom Gunn, that I am in touch with a complete person." —REED WOODHOUSE, *The Boston Book Review*

"A Thom Gunn poem is always a formal animal, and these pieces are really seductions about seductions." —SARA MILLER, *Chicago Tribune*

"*Boss Cupid* contains so many marvelous poems, it can make a reader sorry that conning poetry by heart has fallen out of fashion." —DAVID KIPEN, *San Francisco Chronicle*

"[Gunn's] poetry, no matter its protean shifts over the years . . . has always retained an exciting, even ferocious, quality of exacting obsession about it. This consistency has given Gunn a certain credibility when he has turned his attention to questions of love, or at any rate desire, because writing like this requires an integrity that precludes facile yielding to sentimentality." —JOE KNOWLES, *In These Times*

"By using unpredictable subjects that challenge his reader's assumptions and his own, he's raised the stakes of his artwork." —PETER CAMPION, *The Boston Phoenix*

"[Gunn's] mastery of versification convinces the reader that what he has said can . . . be said in no other way." —DOUGLAS K. CURRIER, *Harvard Review*

"These are poems that span vast distances. They are elegies, retrospective and reflective of times past, and friends and loves long gone. They are forward-looking as well, sometimes playful and even humorous. They sparkle with arresting clarity and beauty . . . Thom Gunn probes the mysteries of life, love and death with brilliance and power." —JIM NAWROCKI, *Bay Area Reporter*

"Gunn's inventive yet controlled formalism, a hallmark of his work, is reminiscent of Renaissance poets like Wyatt and Donne . . . A lithe and lyrical volume by a master of contemporary poetry." —*Kirkus Reviews* (starred review)

"[These are] poems which are at once emotionally profound and exuberant . . . For Gunn, the repetition and variation of love—its forms based on past experience, and its inevitable cycle of growth and decay—are not simply observed phenomena, but constitute a poetics . . . His writing is both topical and substantive—and thus feels very much of the world." —DEVIN JOHNSTON, *Chicago Review*

Thom Gunn

Boss Cupid

THOM GUNN, born in England in 1929, has lived in San Francisco since 1954. His books include *The Man with Night Sweats* (1992), for which he won the Lenore Marshall Poetry Prize, and *Collected Poems* (1994). Among his many honors are the Lila Acheson Wallace/Reader's Digest Award and fellowships from the Guggenheim and MacArthur foundations.

By Thom Gunn

Boss Cupid

Boss Cupid

—

Thom Gunn

Farrar • Straus • Giroux

New York

Farrar, Straus and Giroux
19 Union Square West, New York 10003

Copyright © 2000 by Thom Gunn
All rights reserved
Printed in the United States of America
Originally published in 2000 by Faber and Faber Limited, London
Published in 2000 in the United States by Farrar, Straus and Giroux
First paperback edition, 2001

Library of Congress Cataloging-in-Publication Data
Gunn, Thom.
    Boss Cupid / Thom Gunn.— 1st ed.
        p. cm.
    ISBN 0-374-52771-7 (pbk.)
    I. Title.
    PR6013.U65   B67   2000
    821'.914—dc21   99-057739

Designed by Jonathan D. Lippincott

Contents

"Well, it's a cool queer tale!"
Thomas Hardy,
"Her Second Husband Hears the Story"

1

Duncan

ABAB CDCD rhyme scheme

1

When in his twenties a poetry's full strength
Burst into voice as an unstopping flood,
He let the divine prompting (come at length)
Rushingly bear him any way it would
And went on writing while the Ferry turned
From San Francisco, back from Berkeley too,
And back again, and back again. He learned
You add to, you don't cancel what you do.

sounds almost like Gunn

Between the notebook-margins his pen travelled,
His own lines carrying him in a new mode
To ports in which past purposes unravelled.
So that, as on the Ferry Line he rode,
Whatever his first plans that night had been,
The energy that rose from their confusion
Became the changing passage lived within
While the pen wrote, and looked beyond conclusion.

2

Forty years later, and both kidneys gone;
Every eight hours, home dialysis;
The habit of his restlessness stayed on
Exhausting him with his responsiveness.
After the circulations of one day
In which he taught a three-hour seminar
Then gave a reading clear across the Bay,
And while returning from it to the car

With plunging hovering tread tired and unsteady
Down Wheeler steps, he faltered and he fell
—Fell he said later, as if I stood ready,
"Into the strong arms of Thom Gunn!"

                                        Well well,
The image comic, as I might have known,
And generous, but it turned things round to myth:
He fell across the white steps there alone,
Though it was me indeed that he was with.

I hadn't caught him, hadn't seen in time,
And picked him up where he had softly dropped,
A pillow full of feathers. Was it a rime
He later sought, in which he might adopt
The role of H.D., broken-hipped and old,
Who, as she moved off from the reading-stand,
Had stumbled on the platform but was held
And steadied by another poet's hand?

He was now a posthumous poet, I have said
(For since his illness he had not composed),
In sight of a conclusion, whose great dread
Was closure,

                his life soon to be enclosed
Like the sparrow's flight above the feasting friends,
Briefly revealed where its breast caught their light,
Beneath the long roof, between open ends,
Themselves the margins of unchanging night.

4

The Antagonism

to Helena Shire

The Makers did not make
The muddy winter hardening to privation,
Or cholera in the keep, or frost's long ache
    Afflicting every mortal nation
From lord to villagers in their fading dyes
      —Those who like oxen strained
    On stony clearings of the ground
        From church to sties.

    They sought an utterance,
Or sunshine soluble in institution,
An orthodoxy justified, at once
    The dream and dreamer warmed in fusion,
As in the great Rose Window, pieced from duty,
      Where through Christ's crimson, sun
    Shines on your clothes till they take on
        Value and beauty.

    But carved on a high beam
Far in the vault from the official version
Gape gnarled unChristian heads out of whom stream
    Long stems of contrary assertion,
Shaped leaf ridging their scalps in place of hair.
      Their origins lost to sight,
    As they are too, cast out from light.
        They should despair.

5

What stays for its own sake,
Occulted in the dark, may slip an ending,
Recalcitrant, and strengthened by the ache
    Of winter not for the transcending.
Ice and snow pile the gables of the roof
        Within whose shade they hold,
    Intimate with its slaty cold,
        To Christ aloof.

A Home

Raised, he said, not at home but in a Home. *alliteration*

Bare of associations, words like *bed*,
Breakfast and *birthday* hard eternal forms
As standardized as workbench in the shop
Or regulation metal bunk, with edges
On which you bark your shins because it's there.

Bare of associations.
                            Between the boys
Contact, not loose, not free, consisting mainly
In the wrestling down of slave by slave. Call this
The economy of bruises: threats of worse
Pin you in place, for more convenient handling.
And nothing occurs casually but dirt.

So when a big boy slips you a comic book
Because his heart is big, no other reason,
His unfit action organizes time.

It organizes time through revelation
Of an old prophecy preserved in fragments
Among the boys, a corrupt oral tradition
Concerning the advent of the affections: for
They will be born, and live and prosper too,
Before their inevitable martyrdom.
Your mind starts to prepare a place for them:

And it delights in the cool new-found ease
With which it slips the habitual weary tautness

To enter certain unmapped borderlands.
Waking early
                in the breathing room of beds
To thin unsupervised light, a sanctuary,
You glimpse at last a measure of the future
In which you will seek out similar times
Between times, places between places, thresholds
And fire escapes, buses and laundromats,
To tell in a voice guarded and level, "I
Was raised in a Home," as if it were all over
And the quotidian horror had been mastered.

Sounds orphan like

My Mother's Pride

ABCB

She dramatized herself
Without thought of the dangers.
But "Never pay attention," she said,
"To the opinions of strangers."

And when I stole from a counter,
"You wouldn't accept a present
From a tradesman." But I think I might have:
I had the greed of a peasant.

She was proud of her ruthless wit
And the smallest ears in London.
"Only conceited children are shy."
I am made by her, and undone.

Mothers molding of a child

9

The Gas-poker

Forty-eight years ago
—Can it be forty-eight
Since then?—they forced the door
Which she had barricaded
With a full bureau's weight
Lest anyone find, as they did,
What she had blocked it for.

She had blocked the doorway so,
To keep the children out.
In her red dressing-gown
She wrote notes, all night busy
Pushing the things about,
Thinking till she was dizzy,
Before she had lain down.

The children went to and fro
On the harsh winter lawn
Repeating their lament,
A burden, to each other
In the December dawn,
Elder and younger brother,
Till they knew what it meant.

Knew all there was to know.
Coming back off the grass
To the room of her release,
They who had been her treasures
Knew to turn off the gas,

Take the appropriate measures,
Telephone the police.

One image from the flow
Sticks in the stubborn mind:
A sort of backwards flute.
The poker that she held up
Breathed from the holes aligned
Into her mouth till, filled up
By its music, she was mute.

Suicide. put gas poker in her nose. Blocked door so her children would not find her

A Young Novelist

whose first book was published in the same week that his lover died

You might say a whole life led up to it,
A novel's publication—instances
Gathered and finished, blurbed and jacketed.
You might say also the same life had led
The same week to another rounding off
—Another body of live instances
Rendered succinct, ash in a plastic sack
Tied off severely, obited and let go,
Let go. He lost the wrestler with the smile
Who pinned him to the mat of love for ever,
He'd hoped.
               He doesn't know which way to turn;
Each stroke of fortune will infect the other;
Each is a thought of terrible unrest.

Once on his way to school a schoolboy surfaced
From all of loss to one cold London street
And noticed minute leaves, they were soft points,
Virgin-green, newly eased out of black twigs,
And didn't know, really, what to make of them;
Then turning back to it found he no longer
Knew what to make of the other thing, despair.

Published a novel. His lover died. He lost his touch.

In the Post Office

Saw someone yesterday looked like you did,
Being short with long blond hair, a sturdy kid
Ahead of me in line. I gazed and gazed
At his good back, feeling again, amazed,
That almost envious sexual tension which
Rubbing at made the greater, like an itch,
An itch to steal or otherwise possess
The brilliant restive charm, the boyishness
That half-aware—and not aware enough—
Of what it did, eluded to hold off
The very push of interest it begot,
As if you'd been a tease, though you were not.
I hadn't felt it roused, to tell the truth,
In several years, that old man's greed for youth,
Like Pelias's that boiled him to a soup,
Not since I'd had the sense to cover up
My own particular seething can of worms,
And settle for a friendship on your terms.

Meanwhile I had to look: his errand done,
Without a glance at me or anyone,
The kid unlocked his bicycle outside,
Shrugging a backpack on. I watched him ride
Down 18th Street, rising above the saddle
For the long plunge he made with every pedal,
Expending far more energy than needed.
If only I could do whatever he did,
With him or as a part of him, if I
Could creep into his armpit like a fly,

13

Or like a crab cling to his golden crotch,
Instead of having to stand back and watch.
Oh complicated fantasy of intrusion
On that young sweaty body. My confusion
Led me at length to recollections of
Another's envy and his confused love.

gazing @ the body leave [handwritten annotation]

That Fall after you died I went again
To where I had visited you in your pain
But this time for your—friend, roommate, or wooer?
I seek a neutral term where I'm unsure.
He lay there now. Figuring she knew best,
I came by at his mother's phoned request
To pick up one of your remembrances,
A piece of stained-glass you had made, now his,
I did not even remember, far less want.
To him I felt, likewise, indifferent.

his lovers hospital roommate [handwritten annotation]

"You can come in now," said the friend-as-nurse.
I did, and found him altered for the worse.
But when he saw me sitting by his bed,
He would not speak, and turned away his head.
I had not known he hated me until
He hated me this much, hated me still.
I thought that we had shared you more or less,
As if we shared what no one might possess,
Since in a net we sought to hold the wind.
There he lay on the pillow, mortally thinned,
Weaker than water, yet his gesture proving
As steady as an undertow. Unmoving
In the sustained though slight aversion, grim
In wordlessness. Nothing deflected him,

14

Nothing I did and nothing I could say.
And so I left. I heard he died next day.

The roommate would not speak to him. He died

I have imagined that he still could taste
That bitterness and anger to the last,
Against the roles he saw me in because
He had to: of victor, as he thought I was,
Of heir, as to the cherished property
His mother—who knows why?—was giving me,
And of survivor, as I am indeed,
Recording so that I may later read
Of what has happened, whether between sheets,
Or in post offices, or on the streets.

He has survived while so many have died

Postscript: The Panel

Reciprocation from the dead. Having finished the post office poem, I decide to take a look at the stained-glass panel it refers to, which Charlie made I would say two years before he died. I fish it out from where I have kept it, between a filing cabinet and a small chest of drawers. It has acquired a cobweb, which I brush off when I look at it. In the foreground are a face with oriental features and an arm, as if someone were lying on his stomach: a mysteriously tiered cone lies behind and above him. What I had forgotten is that the picture is surrounded by the following inscription:

The needs of ghosts embarrass the living. A ghost must eat and shit, must pack his body someplace. Neither buyer nor bundle, a ghost has no tally, no readjusting value, no soul counted at a bank.

Is this an excerpt from some Chinese book of wisdom, or is it Charlie himself speaking? When he made the panel, Charlie may have already suspected he had AIDS, but the prescience of the first sentence astonishes me—as it does also that I remembered nothing of the inscription while writing the poem but looked it up immediately on finishing it.

Yes, the needs of him and his friends to "embarrass" me after their deaths. The dead have no sense of tact, no manners, they enter doors without knocking, but I continue to deal with them, as proved by my writing the poem. They pack their bodies into my dreams, they eat my feelings, and shit in my mind. They are no good to me, of no value to me, but I cannot shake them and do not want to. Their story, being part of mine, refuses to reach an end. They present me

with new problems, surprise me, contradict me, my dear, my
everpresent dead.

August 7, 1991

*The post office poem
was a real reflection of
Thom Gunn's life.
his lover, Charlie died of AIDS*

17

The Butcher's Son

Mr Pierce the butcher
Got news his son was missing
About a month before
The closing of the war.
A bald man, tall and careful,
He stood in his shop and found
No bottom to his sadness,
Nowhere for it to stop.
When my aunt came through the door
Delivering the milk,
He spoke, with his quiet air
Of a considerate teacher,
But words weren't up to it,
He turned back to the meat.

Butcher told son was missing because son

The message was in error.
Later that humid summer
At a local high school fete,
I saw, returned, the son
Still in his uniform.
Mr Pierce was not there
But was as if implied
In the son who looked like him
Except he had red hair.
For I recall him well
Encircled by his friends,
Beaming a life charged now
Doubly because restored,
And recall also how

Within his hearty smile
His lips contained his father's
Like a light within the light
That he turned everywhere.

Mr Pierce died of sorrow

An Operation

A couple of policemen dressed
        In plain-clothes best,
Like auto dealers pushing forty,
        Straight and yet sporty,
Sat, one on show and one confined
        To a room behind
The storefront rented in pretence
        It was a fence
—Fly-blown, and on a corner-lot
        Realtors forgot:
So to draw out a neighborhood's
        Just-stolen goods,
And sweep up drifts of petty thieves
        As thick as leaves.

They sent out word and waited while
        The slow shy file
First dribbled in then wouldn't stop.
        The hidden cop
Taped the transactions of the crooks
        Who filled the books
The other kept, practical, blunt,
        Front of a front.

No doubt encouraging some few
        To come into
A school of thieves, a new career,
        Who had stayed clear,
Such cops would view themselves as al-
        legorical,

Unaltered by what they had done
        So long as one,
At a desk somewhere, in the cells,
        Or somewhere else
(In heaven?), could still tell a sting
        From the real thing,
And keep their interesting position
        Above suspicion.

They had grown up with paradox
        And other shocks,
Spaced out with regulation jokes,
        Coffee, and smokes,
In traps that looked like other traps.
        But they got maps.
They'd both been in Vietnam, and knew
        That often you
Have to destroy to liberate.

        And if you wait,
Tilting your chair almost at spill,
        A sort of thrill
Steals upward to the skin maybe,
        Till you are free
To stretch within an innocence
        Born from constraints.
Like spies who fornicate to steal,
        You like the feel,
And sweat into the extended play,
        While day by day
Behind plate-glass flies buzz, get old,
        And cups grow cold.

21

2 cops one is hidden, one out front

Thrill of being a thief

Gunn mentions the war and Vietnam

The Problem

Close to the top
Of an encrusted dark
Converted brownstone West of Central Park
(For this was 1961)
In his room that,
                 a narrow hutch,
Was sliced from some once-cavernous flat,
Where now a window took a whole wall up
And tints were bleached-out by the sun
Of many a summer day,
We lay
         upon his hard thin bed.

He seemed all body, such
As normally you couldn't touch,
Reckless and rough,
One of Boss Cupid's red-
                  haired errand boys
Who couldn't get there fast enough.
Almost like fighting . . .
We forgot about the noise,
But feeling turned so self-delighting
That hurry soon gave way
To give-and-take,
Till each contested, for the other's sake,
To end up not in winning and defeat
But in a draw.

Meanwhile beyond the aureate hair
I saw

A scrap of blackboard with its groove for chalk,
Nailed to a strip of lath
That had half-broken through,
The problem drafted there
                              still incomplete.
After, I found out in the talk
Companion to a cigarette,
That he, turning the problem over yet
In his disorderly and ordered head,
Attended graduate school to teach
And study math,
                              his true
Passion cyphered in chalk beyond my reach.

Two lovers ones
true passion is math

Arethusa Saved

When the god of the river
                    pursues her over Greece
weed-rot on his breath
                    rape on his mind,
at length Arethusa
                    loses her lead,
stops, prays for help
                    from a huntress like herself.

Artemis grants her
                    ground-fog to hide her
and she cowers wetly
                    in condensing cloud
and her own sweat cooling
                    from the cross-country run.
Bubbles itch
                    in her close-cropped hair;
where her foot touches
                    forms a pool, small
but widening quickly;
                    liquid rolls down her,
excessively, really,
                    covering her body
till the body is obscured:
                    a living sheet of water
has clothed then replaced
                    hair, body, and foot.
The river-god roaming
                    round the cloud's circumference

24

sniffing at the edge
        like a dog at a rat-hole
calls out boisterously
        with country-boy bravado
"Arethusa darling
        come out and get screwed."
At last the cloud clears
        —he sees Arethusa
melted to his element,
        a woman of water.
Roaring with joy
        he reverts to river
making to plunge upon her
        and deluge her with dalliance.
But Artemis opened
        many earth-entrances,
cracks underneath her
        hair-thin but deep.
Down them the girl slips
        soaking out of sight
before his glassy stare
        —to be conducted through darkness
to another country,
        Sicily, where she springs
(fountain Arethuse)
        as virgin stream presiding
over pastoral hymn
        with intact hymen,
to be figured on medals
        flanked by fish,
hair caught in a net
        whom the god never netted.

25

[handwritten margin notes: Arethusa is being chased by the god of the river. Artemis hides her in a thick foggy cloud. Quickly it turns to pools till water covers Arethusa but Arethusa makes a plunge @ "Arethusa" God of river sending her to sicily where she opens up a crack in the earth sending her to sicily where she becomes a spring. Cloud clears.]

Arethusa Raped

Unmixed
       Alpheus
behind, Arethusa still
leading, they dart
through sea as if
comet pursued comet

through dark tons
barely swaying
    they shoot,
silvery currents,
until at last
brought short on
despair or the shock
of land again, she
stops, he closes,
they join in coral
woods
        water
to water.

And later, bubbling
from earth
    a fountain.

Though a cup
dropped in his stream
in Arcadia bob
a week later to
the surface of a spring

in Ortygia, that spring
has her name, for he
has entered her
meanings, his water
subdued to hers

in the ground she led him to

ground of her goddess.

water mixed with water brought forth fountain

Arachne

What is that bundle hanging from the ceiling
Unresting even now with constant slight
Drift in the breeze that breathes through rooms at night?
Can it be something, then, that once had feeling,
A girl, perhaps, whose skill and pride and hope
Strangled against each other in the rope?

I think it is a tangle of despair
As shapeless as a bit of woven nest,
Blackened and matted, quivering without rest
At the mercy of the movements of the air
Where half-lodged in, half-fallen from the hedge
It hangs tormented at a season's edge.

What an exact artificer she had been!
Her daintiness and firmness are reduced
To lumpy shadow that the dark has noosed.
Something is changing, though. Movements begin
Obscurely as the court of night adjourns,
A tiny busyness at the centre turns.

So she spins who was monarch of the loom,
Reduced indeed, but she lets out a fine
And delicate yet tough and tensile line
That catches full day in the little room,
Then sways minutely, suddenly out of sight,
And then again the thread invents the light.

Enough

Here is the bed she lay on, look, a double
Though she slept by herself, divorced and rich,
No longer having to seem like a wife.
A partner was not really worth the trouble.
Here is the futon's yellowing grey on which
She spent a strait third of her later life.

She liked the padded firmness, as ungiving
As she herself, or floormats at the gym
She attended three times weekly to keep fit.
The futon was in style for healthy living;
But from pure ignorance—or self-punishing whim?—
She got up without ever turning it.

Yet it did give. Look here, now she is gone.
She always kept to the one side of the bed,
And here her body's obstinate impress
Bore down the surface she curled nightly on.
It must have never come into her head
To lie diagonally or move across.

She dug a small mould not to be exceeded,
And rested in the unexacting habit.
Defiant hollow in the greyish stuff!
Here she lay sour, unneeding and unneeded,
Like a divorcee, like an aging rabbit
On stale straw, in its hutch. Enough, enough.

The "life" of a woman lost to love

29

Cat Island

Cats met us at
the landing-place
reclining in the sun
to check us in
with a momentary glance,
concierges
of a grassy island.
(Attila's Throne,
the Devil's Bridge,
and "the best Byzantine
church in the world,"
long saints admonitory
on kiln-like inner walls.)
And lunch in a shady court
where cats now
systematically worked
the restaurant, table
by table, gazing into eyes
pleading "I'm hungry
and I'm cute," reaching
front paws up to knees
and always getting
before zeroing in
on the next table, same
routine, same result.

Sensible bourgeois
wild-cats working
with the furred impudence
of those who don't pretend

not true

to be other than whores,
they give you not
the semblance of love
but simply
a look at their beauty
in return for food.
They lack, too,
the prostitute's self-pity,
being beyond pity.
And we lack
what they have.

Difference between house & street cats

Nights with the Speed Bros.

Lovers, not brothers, whatever they might say
That brilliant first night, being equally blond,
Equally catlike as they reached beyond
The tropes of dalliance to the meat of play.

What I still keep from our long lamp-lit climb
Through gallant and uncertain fantasy
Are marginal gaps a window granted me,
When I removed myself from time to time.

I gazed at moonrise over the wide streets,
A movie letting out, a crowd's dilations,
Bars, clocks, the moon ironic at her stations:
By these the window paragraphed our feats.

Then dawn developed in the room, but old.
. . . I thought (unmitigated restlessness
Clawing its itch): "I gave up sleep for this?"
Dead leaves replaced the secret life of gold.

A System

PCP, or Angel Dust

It's not spread pupils and aphasic speech
And hovering walk that matter, matter at all,
They are mere symptoms, like the howls that reach
Through membranes of our sleep, through floor and wall,
To summon us: we'll find him as before,
His look of horror fading to surprise,
Squatting ass-naked in some corridor,
A ringing in his ears like distant cries.

It's that he in effect closed his life down,
A store gone out of business—and who knows
The turning point, for the delighted town
Once jostled through those doors now forced to close.
And EVERYTHING MUST GO. Everything went.
Family, friends, like discontinued styles.
He threw away his gift, and will not paint,
Listening to air pour through the vacant aisles.

He dreams at the center of a closed system,
Like the prison system, or a system of love,
Where folktale, recipe, and household custom
Refer back to the maze that they are of.

He cannot, though, be said to live alone.
Something is there that, unseen, unofficial,
Shares bed and drafty building, something known
By chemical smell and dry three-fold initial.
It shows him things that next day he'll forget:

Effects of PCP

33

He'll fire it up to find out what they were;
It takes a bully's pleasure of him, yet
Represents freedom like a first affair.

Never never again another weaning
Says the lost son, smoking to recollect
The elusive texture of ineffable meaning . . .
With exits boarded, how can he reflect,
Lying inside it, his closed system, maze
Of solitary cell, exercise yard,
Office, canteen, laced up with passage ways?

And if he did unpick it, if he dared
Resume the self—structure would come apart,
His room a drawer where string is kept, found thing
Scribbled with pothooks, he the tightening heart
That knots the tangles in ten kinds of string.

SAY NO TO DRUGS

Sequel

We looked for two recoveries, as if one
Might take place independent of the other.
Here was a knot that would not come undone,
For all the strings in it had pulled together,
Tight from the lover's death, tight from the drug
That seemed to ease the loss by such distortion
As to convert the pain of every tug
To flashes lighting scenes of disproportion.
In his socks hurrying up the rainy street
To Tank Hill, where they ran, their old direction,
He could be barely checked, so sure he'd meet
The lost one up there, *Jim's astral projection.*

Then eighteen months had passed and he had gone
To France—no smuggler, planning this vacation
Without the powder much depended on
(At least that seems the likely explanation)—
And, almost unawares, while driving through
The valley of the Loire, shrugged off his mourning,
His other habit falling from him too
At the same instant, without thought or warning.
His visionary grief at last undone,
Relaxed by wine and castles, losing, loosened,
The knot elided by the touch of sun,
Till (*here I am!*) he bobbed up in the present.
Though, sitting among tones of daylight glassed
In polished dented tables and old seating
He now dwelt on a subtler larger past,
Recovery seemed an art obvious as eating.
For some innate brutality could still

35

Resume the push toward health, call on resources
To displace the hurt memory thus, and fill
The void with its own lovely heartless forces.

The body had nursed his injured psyche well.
We saw a life recovered in the middle,
To be resumed as, for a ripening spell,
He entered on a carefree sunflecked idyll,
Relishing it. With cheerful undiscerning
He volunteered at last: "I can't pretend
I didn't enjoy myself this last weekend."
And we rejoiced to think his luck returning.

learned not to live constant mourning

Shit

an essay on Rimbaud

The marvellous boy, in his sweet sticky ardor,
Grabbed M. Paul beneath the café table
And growing harder (his poetry grew harder)
Pumped him as thoroughly as he was able.

The older poet, master of sweet sounds,
Couldn't keep up with all this penile strumming
Of the enthusiastic vagabond's.
He always felt religious after coming.

[handwritten: In a cafe?!?]

The boy was bolder. Hair crawling with lice,
Smoked a foul pipe, it was deliberate,
Cracked poetry readings open, far from nice,
His favorite saying shit, and he meant shit.

[handwritten: ← Icky boy]

Coursed after meaning, meaning of course to trick it,
Across the lush green meadows of his youth,
To the edge of the unintelligible thicket
Where truth becomes the same place as untruth,

And trapped it between the two, awful suspension,
Its whiskers quivering through the Romantic mist,
In terror that had stripped it of intention.
He was as cool as a vivisectionist.

For then he ate it, he ate meaning live,
Ate all provincial France, the pasturing herd

And village-girls he once had thought to wive.
His shit was poetry: alchemy of the word.

He levitated, swooning from sheer power.
"Only I have the key," he came to state,
Dreaming that he had reached the highest tower,
But woke on hard stones. Those he also ate.

Till in the end he lost words; and his faeces
Came just from what he ate with fork and knife;
And subsequently too he fell to pieces,
Losing a leg here, there a life.

The Dump

He died, and I admired
the crisp vehemence
of a lifetime reduced to
half a foot of shelf space.
But others came to me saying,
we too loved him,
let us take you to
the place of our love.
So they showed me
everything, everything—
a cliff of notebooks
with every draft and erasure
of every poem he
published or rejected,
thatched already
with webs of annotation.
I went in further and saw
a hill of matchcovers
from every bar or restaurant
he'd ever entered. Trucks
backed up constantly,
piled with papers, awaited
by archivists with shovels;
forklifts bumped through
trough and valley
to adjust the spillage.
Here odors of rubbery sweat
intruded on the pervasive
smell of stale paper,
no doubt from the mound

of his collected sneakers.
I clambered up the highest
pile and found myself
looking across not history
but the vistas of a steaming
range of garbage
reaching to the coast itself. Then
I lost my footing! and was
carried down on a soft
avalanche of letters, paid bills,
sexual polaroids, and notes
refusing invitations, thanking
fans, resisting scholars.
In nightmare I slid
no ground to stop me,

until I woke at last
where I had napped beside
the precious half-foot. Beyond that,
nothing, nothing at all.

Someone deleted
a poet
their legacy

Jokes, etc.

For the Late R.F.
Without a net, eh? Orpheus then is
Mere player in a game of tennis?

To Another Poet
You scratch my back, I like your taste it's true,
But, Mister, I won't do the same for you,
Though you have asked me twice. I have taste too.

Conversion
Improbable and rapid and deep-felt,
Betrayal is the other way it's spelt.

Eastern Europe
(February, 1990)
"The iron doors of history" give at last,
And we walk through them from a rigid past.
Free! free! we can do anything we choose
—Eat at McDonald's, persecute the Jews.

Epitaph
(carved in the AIDS Memorial Grove, Golden Gate Park)

Walker within this circle, pause.
Although they all died of one cause,
Remember how their lives were dense
With fine, compacted difference.

Ace
An AWOL sailor as he drinks
Recalls a recent joke he's heard:
He who can barely read a word
Tells me the riddle of the Sphinx.

Hedonism
After the Scythians, how advance
In the pursuit of happiness?
They went around in leather pants,
And every night smoked cannabis.

The 1970s
There are many different varieties of New Jerusalem,
Political, pharmaceutical—I've visited most of them.
But of all the embodiments ever built, I'd only return to one,
For the sexual New Jerusalem was by far the greatest fun.

Saturday Night

I prowl the labyrinthine corridors
    And have a sense of being underground
As in a mine . . . dim light, the many floors,
    The bays, the heat, the tape's explosive sound.
People still entering, though it is 3 a.m.,
    Stripping at lockers and, with a towel tied round,
Stepping out hot for love or stratagem,
    Pausing at thresholds (wonder never ends),
Peering at others, as others peer at them
    Like people in shelters searching for their friends
Among the group come newest from the street.
    And in each room a different scene attends:
Friends by the bedful, lounging on one sheet,
    Playing cards, smoking, while the drugs come on,
Or watching the foot-traffic on the beat,
    Ready for every fresh phenomenon.
This was the Barracks, this the divine rage
    In 1975, that time is gone.
All here, of any looks, of any age,
    Will get whatever they are looking for,
Or something close, the rapture they engage
    Renewable each night.
                                If, furthermore,
Our Dionysian experiment
    To build a city never dared before
Dies without reaching to its full extent,
    At least in the endeavor we translate
Our common ecstasy to a brief ascent
    Of the complete, grasped, paradisal state
Against the wisdom pointing us away.

What hopeless hopefulness. I watch, I wait—
The embraces slip, and nothing seems to stay
    In our community of the carnal heart.
Some lose conviction in mid-arc of play,
    Their skin turns numb, they dress and will depart:
The perfect body, lingering on goodbyes,
    Cannot find strength now for another start.
Dealers move in, and murmuring advertise
    Drugs from each doorway with a business frown.
Mattresses lose their springs. Beds crack, capsize,
    And spill their occupants on the floor to drown.
Walls darken with the mold, or is it rash?
    At length the baths catch fire and then burn down,
And blackened beams dam up the bays of ash.

The collapse of something from the past

American Boy

I do not seek you out
    For if I do
You say I might get tired of you.
    To think I was afraid
You'd be the one to tire while we both still
    Warm to the naked thrill
Precisely of that strangeness that has made
    For such self-doubt.

    I hated those old men
        With turkey-necks
And undiminished love of sex,
    The curtains of their skin
Tripping them up at their incautious play,
    When out of torpor they
Had woken as ambitious as if in
    Their prime again.

    Now I myself am old
        We calculate
Our games for such and such a date.
    Like bicoastal romance,
In which one night a quarter is the most
    Spared to the other coast,
Ours thrives as we stretch out our ignorance:
    Men of the world.

    Affectionate young man,
        Your wisdom feeds
My dried-up impulses, my needs,

With energy and juice.
Expertly you know how to maintain me
  At the exact degree
Of hunger without starving. We produce
  What warmth we can.

Young man stands
for ... something

Painting by Vuillard

Two dumpy women with buns were drinking coffee
In a narrow kitchen—at least I think a kitchen
And I think it was whitewashed, in spite of all the shade.
They were flat brown, they were as brown as coffee.
Wearing brown muslin? I really could not tell.
How I loved this painting; they had grown so old
That everything had got less complicated,
Brown clothes and shade in a sunken whitewashed kitchen.

But it's not like that for me: age is not simpler
Or less enjoyable, not dark, not whitewashed.
The people sitting on the marble steps
Of the national gallery, people in the sunlight,
A party of handsome children eating lunch
And drinking chocolate milk, and a young woman
Whose T-shirt bears the defiant word WHATEVER,
And wrinkled folk with visored hats and cameras
Are vivid, they are not browned, not in the least,
But if they do not look like coffee they look
As pungent and startling as good strong coffee tastes,
Possibly mixed with chicory. And no cream.

2

GOSSIP

Famous Friends

Could never place him.
But I'd go into
BAR on 2nd Avenue
and there he was, face
lighting up, helpful
silly and eager, yes
started again
and now unstoppable
on an expressway
of talk, fast and funny, but
after half an hour
I'd edge away.

J.J.,
he said, J.J.,
that's my name.
Talked, that time,
of getting something published
—So you write! I said.
Why, didn't you know,
his smile triumphant,
I was
Frank O'Hara's last lover.

Didn't see him again.
It was like having met
—years afterwards—
Fanny Brawne
full of bounce, or

Degen, the conceited
baker's boy.

No it wasn't.

Rather, it was like having met
Nell Gwyn,
on the way down,
good-natured, losing weight,
still chatting about spaniels.

A GI in 1943

He melted into his
uniform, the blond hair
uniform too
rough animal stubble above
the undisturbed beauty
of the farm boy's face.
Boy flesh
in a man's tunic,
the hands too
regulation-pink.
A standard presented
at age thirteen, coming back
from rowing-practice
on the Thames.
Nowadays I see
forward boys in backward caps
armored in hide that
adorns to hide
every fallibility,
cruelty or awkwardness
with the smooth look
of power. Power
as beauty, beauty
power, that
is all my cock knew or
cared to know, taught
by the focusing eye, as it
isolated the god
from the crowd, surveyed
from the bus-top

drafted

that May afternoon in
Richmond, never seen close,
never seen again, and
has learned nothing
fresh in fifty-three years.

Front Bar of the *Lone Star*

Fat flesh egg
400 lbs of him
set firmly on
the toothpick stool.
Fat, fat.
Styles change:
use a new word
and what you see is new.
Great not gross now,
chubby not fat.
Great flesh daddy,
chubby-chaser's delight.
Contempt or pity
of twenty years
melted in admiration.

change of language

Some feet distant,
what slender youth!
gaze fixed on
this dream of quantity.
Encouraged, squeezes
to the adjacent stool:
just enough room
for flirting from.

The point of the heart-
shaped Raphael face
gave way to
the sporty chin
of the Gibson girl.

Styles change.
The democracy of it:
eventually everyone
can hope for a turn
at being wanted.

Fat girl
skinny boy likes her

To Donald Davie in Heaven

I was reading Auden—But I thought
you didn't like Auden, I said.
Well, I've been reading him again,
and I like him better now, you said.
That was what I admired about you
your ability to regroup
without cynicism, your love of poetry
greater
than your love of consistency.

As in an unruffled fish-pond
the fish draw to whatever comes
thinking it something to feed on

*feed on stuff
for poetry
everything*

there was always something to feed on
your appetite unslaked
for the fortifying and tasty
events of reading.

I try to think of you now
nestling in your own light,
as in Dante, singing to God
the poet and literary critic.

As you enter among them,
the other thousand surfaced glories
—those who sought honour
by bestowing it—

sing at your approach
Lo, one who shall increase our loves.

But maybe less druggy,
a bit plainer,
more Protestant.

"J kinda funny

A Los Angeles Childhood

My stepfather sat on the can
while I was taking a shower,
he would read the paper, but when I got out,
towelling myself, into his stink,
he'd look over at me.

I was eight. Whenever my mother was out,
it was time for punishment,
for whatever I'd done,
he'd take off his belt and then
wale into me, then he'd fuck me.
I hated him! Sometimes
when his car was there but hers wasn't,
I'd hide and not go home,
but sometimes I would.
It happened a lot but never
when she was there. Later,
I said if he went on doing it
I'd tell her, and he stopped.
He worked in a factory
he had a terrible death
he had multiple sclerosis.

My mother
was a cruel woman.
One of my brothers pissed in bed
so she tied him to a high chair
with a sign on him saying what he did,
in the yard right by
where all the kids went to school

so they could all see.
Me, I couldn't spell,
so she made me kneel in a corner
on kidney beans. I spell words
just like they sound, I get understood.

First chance I got, I enlisted.
She's still alive.
I don't go see her.

The Artist as an Old Man

Vulnerable because
naked because
his own model.

Muscled and veined, not
a bad old body
for an old man.
The face vulnerable too,
its loosened folds
huddled against
the earlier outline: beneath
the assertion of nose
still riding the ruins
you observe the down-
turned mouth: and
above it,
the assessing glare
which might be read as
I've got the goods on you
asshole and I'll expose you.
The flat palette knife
in his right hand, and
the square palette itself
held low in the other
like a shield,
he faces off
the only appearance
reality has and makes it
doubly his. He
looks into

his own eyes
or it might be yours
and his attack on the goods
repeats the riddle
or it might be
answers it:

> *Out of the eater*
> *came forth meat*
> *and out of the strong*
> *came forth sweetness.*

The little cousin dashed in
from her friends outside:
"Mother, what
do we think about God?"
My aunt's brisk answer:
"We think God is silly."

My cousin dashed back
with the news.

Life experience?

Classics

Bartending is a branch
of show business. Your bartender
can flirt as heavy as he wants
without danger of being
taken for real, thanks
to the wide spread
of wood between
him and the customer. There
are stars of course and
bit players. Tony   —> cute
was known for the little
folded notes he pushed across
to cute numbers from out of town.
Boy, was his spelling bizarre.
Likewise his propositions.
But Scorpio   ——> creepy but
was also a porn star, his   —> still seductive
equipment as well known
as his face probably.
Behind the bar he wore
one of those net shirts
so his nipples poked
through two of the holes.
It was a pity about
the sibilance, but
I could have killed
for a chance to chew
on those jumbo tits.

7 a.m. in the bar
that opened at 6.
He's been up all night and so
(by definition) have
the other early birds.
Electrically tired.
"Well I've been away
the last three years."
The tip-off: others
would say
where. Sheds his shirt
to play pool.
Prison physique, prison
tattoos, the leisurely Gothic
characters across his shoulder-
blades spelling
BRAVADO.
   Bored
with last night's provider,
he cut out, taking
the cowboy boots, since
they did fit. He waits
and looks around him.

Thinks
of getting a beeper.

Hi

Hi,
I'm Hugo, your
waiter for tonight.
I will compose
the man you expect
out of apron and
native wit, even
my errors included,
solicitously
wiping spilled wine
from your lovely sleeve,
deeply charming you,
as if charm could be deep.
I may seduce
your wife, and you
will trust me. I
found the form but
I made up the content.
Each new sonnet
a plot against the sonnet.

Voice of a waiter

Coffee on Cole

On the outside
tables and inside, they
sit drinking coffee.
Most are male, some
writing seriously
—you can tell they are serious
from their hiking boots.
Clothes for the job.
The male job. (Where
do women write?
It seems not here.)
These write
to write,
        to capture
the green lights of the fly
on a half-eaten
bear-claw, and I
emulate them
who in their purity
have achieved
nothing, though
when I was like them
I emulated those
who had already bound
their choices up.

A cup of coffee
can last hours.
You start
by playing a part

in a place you hope is
holy and hospitable,
trying if nothing
else turns up
a surreal account of
the way the muse
avoids returning your calls.

Letters from Manhattan

1
Hello T.G.
It's snowing again. Two days
after last month's blizzard I went
to the cruise section of Central Park.
I found a young Mexican guy
and we had j.o. sex under a bridge.
(Does that make me a troll?)

2
I'll take Latin
Manhattan.

*were these
sent to him*

3
At Yankee Stadium
the line in the men's room
was so long, four guys
broke into
the unlit janitor's closet
and stood around
the mop-sink pissing
—three beer-bellied slobs
and one right-on hot
Puerto Rican teen
emerged from the small dark room.
Forget pee-shy
I got pee-catatonia.

4

I seek a potent mix
of toughness and tenderness in men.
The paradigm
being the weeping wrestler.

5

The snow was over
2 ft high, but someone
had dug out trails
all through the Rambles.

——————

Save the word
empathy, sweetheart,
for your freshman essays.
Doesn't it make
a rather large
claim? Think you can
syphon yourself
into another human
as, in the movie,
the lively boy-ghosts
pour themselves
down the ear-holes
of pompous older men?
Don't try it. Only
Jesus could do it and he
probably didn't exist.
Try "sympathy." With that
your isolated self may
split a cloak with the beggar,
slip a pillow under the head
of the arrested man, hold tight
the snag-toothed hostler with red hair.

Convergence

She might be
a child of Weathermen
sporting that short hair
with a boy's parting
as defiance of their
tangled romanticism.

She
doesn't eat
dead cat to toughen her
for the coming
class war,
the coming is over,
she has read Marx
but prefers John
Ashbery,
       she goes
to clubs in the City
and drives her friends
back to Berkeley
           fueled
on wit and risk
and Ecstasy.

       She lives
one fine protest
against you might say
ethnic purity—
her eyes, her facial
structure, her name, they

point from different directions
toward a vivacious
harmony, Hawaiian,
Irish, Cherokee,
Jewish, Chinese, these
for a start.

—It must make it
awfully difficult,
said the English visitor,
all that blood
fighting amongst itself.

Oh!
        she had
failed to notice.

the melting pot

73

Blues for the New Year, 1997

My dealer left town
(sounds like a song).

Had a date with
a certain man, but
he got pneumonia.
I guess it's off.

Bad day/year?

Storm after storm
bowls in
off the Pacific.

Pale and sleepy on
his Tenderloin mattress.
He has different-
colored eyes and nothing
about him quite matches.
A challenge.

Oh, it's just New
Year's. I'm
not superstitious:
the year may turn out
very rewarding. Anyway
I'm sixty-seven,
and have high blood pressure,
and probably shouldn't
be doing speed at all.

Let's reschedule!

Aubade

Kinder than you will own,
pleasing yourself you say
through pleasing me

till a desolating
change of light
steals into the room
rosyfingered orderly
thinning out
our packed intensities
of night

    Already
you turn away, thoughts
on the future.

The Search

Lookin to hook up
with a younger guy from E Bay.
You: cab driver's build,
lots of attitude. Me:
hi self esteem,
lo tolerance for
anything not me.
Am forty-eight, work out,
classic abs, uncut.
Wanna deconstruct,
man on man? Let's do
lunch and each other.
Leave #. Movie stars
OK, insensitivity a big +

want ad

Office Hours

these big handsome
sweaty boys
with their goatees
and skateboards

these sharp chic
ironic girls
with brisk hairstyles
and subtle tattoos

we sit close
but sexuality
is grandly deflected
because the ground
on which we meet
is Bunting's flexible
unrepetitive line
or Wyatt's careful
sidestepping of danger

they attract
me I make them
laugh we
talk about
the way people
talk about
sweat and danger
we do not flirt with
one another
it is a poet

we flirt with
together

78

Stories of bar-fights,
boasts of glory.
That's the old cat
talking now, that one
with the tattered ear.
"Yeah," he says,
"I was passing the wash house
back of the farm kitchen,
where I sometimes got handouts,
and there's this passel of kittens
in a basket, mewing
their fuckn heads off. Well,
some of them were male,
future toms. You know I had
to do something about that.
So I dove in, checking
them males like I always can
(call it a talent), and I bit off
the heads of the ah
competition. Heh, the little gals
I left to grow up a bit.
Then there was that time,
I was still in the Marines,
facing a bar full of sailors
with jest a broken bottle . . ."
Vaunting voice grates
on and on, nobody listening, until
he has drunk himself
asleep. No longer deadly,

no longer dashing, nothing but
a shabby old tabby.

Drunkard @
a bar

First saw him
on the street in front, in the
bar's garbage, identifying
unfinished beers and swigging
off what was left of them,
shameless and exuberant,
remarking in friendly fashion
"It's a doggy dog world."
Charming error. He
had little idea of his looks
caught on a brief sill
between youthful lean times
and blowziness to come,
and too unfocused to try
hustling more than beer
and a night out of the rain.
Later, circling vaguely
the bar's deep dark inside,
"Hitched up from New Orleans,"
he said. "Here, wanna feel it?"
It was already out
pushed soft into my hand. It was
a lovely gift to offer an old
stranger
                without conditions
a present from New Orleans
in a doggy dog world.

3

Troubadour

songs for Jeffrey Dahmer

Hitch-hiker

Oh do not leave me now.
All that I ever wanted is compressed
In your sole body. As you turn to go
I know that I must keep you, and know how,
For I must hold the ribbed arch of your chest
    And taste your boyish glow.

The strain, the strain returns
Of my desire to own the elusive one
I have not even possessed. Though you recoil
At my first touch, your flesh yields when it learns
That love must be ensnared while on the run,
    For later it will spoil.

I thought that you were gone,
But you are here and will remain with me.
Your long hair floods the pillow that we share
Across the mattress we lie quietly on.
I trust your mute consent in which I'm free
    To strip your body bare.

My song in each reprise
Will follow this first order, strain by strain:
Strain of desire, and hope, and worst of all

The strain of feeling loss, but after these
Strain of the full possession once again
That has a dying fall.

Iron Man

That sullen moody summer when it rained each day
I sat in my room, sat in the kennel of my inaction,
With few abilities, my parents were away
Getting divorced I think, I gnawed dissatisfaction.

The fridge was broke, but I had booze, I was seventeen,
And half-drunk all day, all of the day I masturbated.
My solace was a picture in a magazine,
A standard out of *Iron Man,* muscles inflated.

His eyes stared up, I memorized the amorous scowl,
I played with myself, played with myself, absorbed in study
Of his tan body burnished like a basted fowl,
Biceps and pecs, what could I do with such a buddy.

And good enough to eat. I was hungry for a life,
Life of my own, life I could own, as cock was my witness.
Later maybe some fraulein might become my wife.
But next day I would buy the latest *Muscle and Fitness.*

87

The Visible Man

Now I can count on you.
People are restless and they move too much,
But you no longer have a young man's heart
Hot for experience without review,
Pumping responses to the latest touch:
      We do not need to part.

      Yet nothing lasts, you know.
I tell you what, there is a place divides
The house's structure, hidden at the center.
If I show you that crawl-space, you must show
The inmost secrets to me that skin hides.
      Here, I will help you enter.

A Borrowed Man

Loose in the twilight slot between
Floor and foundation, I have seen
Such things committed in your name,
　Iron Man, Only Love,
As would not be allowed above
Or contemplated without shame.

I beg from memory each limb,
Each body-part that spoiled with time:
The sidelong hungry look of him,
From him a stammer, from another
A single bicep blue with Mother,
From one a scalp, with hair's regalia,
From one large hands and lazy grin,
From someone reddened genitalia,
And last, the image of the chest
From my original conquest,
The cage once tented in its skin,
Now great free-standing ribs that I'm
Leaving as bare bone rather than
Refleshing, best part of the best,
　Only Love, Iron Man.

But these are nothing, and I head
Off to the kitchen, where instead
I'll find more tangible effects
Than what the memory collects.

I rove round it to gratify
    Iron love . . .
And if the sight that meets my eye,
The cold cuts on the metal shelf
    (Only man),
Stumbles me till I hesitate,
Yet I can count on the revival
Of such heat as will concentrate
My scattered force into a self
Defined by both the circumstances
And the accompanying fancies
To all of my orgasms past,
Long-dried, or wiped-off, but now massed
Steeply through memory's survival.
    (Iron Man, Only Love.)
They mount, and break, and in recapture
Flood me with rightness of my rapture.

Final Song

I fell into myself
nothing could raise me now

a head stood on the shelf
beside lard in a cup
the questioning face gazed up
locked in its own surmise
the abbreviated eyes
the nostril hairs the brow
perplexing from the past
the mouth's sardonic twist

could not be said to last
or even to exist
though fresh and well-maintained
the skin a healthy brown

I stared at each black eye

only myself remained
in which I wandered lost
by my monotonous coast
beneath my sky a sky
a clouded sky closed down

burdened by my erection

notice punctuation

91

a face stared from a shelf
unreadable on guard

connection disconnection
between headcheese and lard

only one self remained
fresh credibly maintained.

Coffee Shop

I recognize them in the booth,
Weak, greedy, lovely in their greed, *(first date)*
Shakily locking mouth to mouth,
Where mutually they start to feed.

The first kiss prelude to a tale
Where neither entertains suspicion
How they might change, how they might fail.
Nothing can shake this recognition:

The moment that they break into
The closed-up house of love; they slip
From room to room and, as they do,
Adventure through a companionship

Thick with their projects. What is best,
They know they'll not be bored again,
Proud to return the interest
They get and think they can sustain.

They drag the stocky shutters apart
And let light in upon the floor,
The dance-ground of the active heart,
Where they could play for ever more,

The lovers tangled in mid-phrase,
As if obstructed tongues might say:
"We are the same in different ways,
We are different in the same way." *(again repetition)*

Rapallo

Before the heavy hotel sink
I lost myself a minute.
I paused as people do who think,
And gazed at what was in it.

Rinsed from my swimming trunks, the sand
Wavered down grain by grain
To settle at the bottom stunned,
Distinct on thick porcelain.

As if my happiness was tired
And sought that strange mild pause,
It still observantly endured
And yet forgot its cause.

But then from habit I looked round
For what I thought it lacked.
Of course: for without you as ground,
How could it stay intact?

Turned to miss you, amnesiac,
I was restored when you
Across the floor were given back,
—Changing for dinner too,

For those discoveries still ahead
To match those of our play
Upon the beach where we had led
All of a spacious day.

That summer I was twenty-three,
You about twenty-one,
We hoped to live together, as we
(Not to be smug) have done.

If in four decades matter-of-factly
Coming to be resigned
To separate beds was not exactly
What we then had in mind,

Something of our first impetus,
Something of what we planned
Remains of what was given us
On the Rapallo sand.

Against our house of floors and beams
A mannerless wind strains
Down from the North, and cold rain streams
Across the window panes.

The structure creaks we hold together.
Water blurs all detail.
This wood will speak beneath worse weather
Yet than the Yukon's hail.

reflection or part

In Trust

You go from me
　In June for months on end
To study equanimity
　Among high trees alone;
I go out with a new boyfriend
And stay all summer in the city where
　Home mostly on my own
　I watch the sunflowers flare.

　You travel East
　To help your relatives.
The rainy season's start, at least,
　Brings you from banishment:
And from the hall a doorway gives
A glimpse of you, writing I don't know what,
　Through winter, with head bent
　In the lamp's yellow spot.

　To some fresh task
　Some improvising skill
Your face is turned, of which I ask
　Nothing except the presence:
Beneath white hair your clear eyes still
Are candid as the cat's fixed narrowing gaze
　—Its pale-blue incandescence
　In your room nowadays.

　Sociable cat:
　Without much noise or fuss
We left the kitchen where he sat,

And suddenly we find
He happens still to be with us,
In this room now, though firmly faced away,
Not to be left behind,
Though all the night he'll stray.

As you began
You'll end the year with me.
We'll hug each other while we can,
Work or stray while we must.
Nothing is, or will ever be,
Mine, I suppose. No one can hold a heart,
But what we hold in trust
We do hold, even apart.

To Cupid

You make desire seem easy.
                                So it is:
Your service perfect freedom to enjoy
Fresh limitations. I've watched you in person
Wait for the light and relish the delay
Revving the engine up before you spurt
Out of the intersection.

                                How all your servants
Compose their amorous scripts—scripts of confinement,
Scripts of displacement, scripts of delay, and scripts
Of more delay. Your own Fabrice so hankered
After the distance of his prison cell
He managed to regain it, for the sake
Of viewing her, the jailer's daughter, daily—
But at a window, but among her birds.
Of course they could not touch. In later life
They touched, they did touch, but in darkness only.

When I switched off my light I was dog-tired
But for some minutes held off sleep: I heard
The pleasant sound of voices from next door
Through windows open to the clement darkness.
A dinner for the couple one floor up,
Married today. I hardly had the time
Before falling away, to relish it,
The sociable human hum, easy and quiet
As the first raindrops in the yard, on bushes,
Heard similarly from bed. Chatting, the sounds
Of friendliness and feeding often broken

By laughter. It's consoling, Mr Love, *epithet?*
That such conviviality is also
One more obedience to your behest,
The wedding bed held off by the wedding feast.

Good will within delay within good will.
And Cupid, devious master of our bodies,
You were the source then of my better rest.

Front Door Man

Prelude
You! first thing at the door
In a rumpled grass-green shirt,
Wraithlike, saying you need
To sleep at the end of four
Tumultuous nights on speed.

You don't feel anecdotal,
Give me a weary grin,
And eat three plates of Total.

The shirt's now on the floor
When I put you in my bed
And at once you slump inert.
I look in now and then
And marvel: your hollowness
Almost perceptibly fed
And filling out again.

Thus breath by breath it seems
You take form, you recover
The strength to do it over,
Resume the cycle, at best
Regaining through such extremes
The ability to rest.

Is my thought love or duty?
I most want to protect—
To care for you like a mother
Although when I am faced

By your full daunting beauty
I barely can reject
The impulse of quite other.

Plaint →ep thet
Love-god, Cupid, why
Did you have to send me him
That weekday afternoon,
Andy, this big young blond
Pointedly grabbing himself
As he looked me in the eye
Along bar and pool-table
From the window-niche beyond,
Like a smiling sexual saint?

What on earth can I hope?
This, Cupid, is my plaint.
I seem to be more and more
Attracted by the unstable
Bright and accident-prone
Homeless, who look a lot
Like hustlers but are not.
And in this I am shown
A cycle of my own.

Are you appointing me
To hold him safe tonight
Or use him for my delight?
If *he* doesn't know why he
Comes back to my front door,
How, Cupid, can I cope?

A Wood near Athens

1

The traveler struggles through a wood. He is lost.
The traveler is at home. He never left.
He seeks his way on the conflicting trails,
Scribbled with light.

                I have been this way before.

Think! the land here is wooded still all over.
An oak snatched Absalom by his bright hair.
The various trails of love had led him there,
The people's love, his father's, and self-love.

What if it does indeed come down to juices
And organs from whose friction we have framed
The obsession in which we live, obsession I call
The wood preceding us as we precede it?
We thought we lived in a garden, and looked around
To see that trees had risen on all sides.

2

It is ridiculous, ridiculous,
And it is our main meaning.

                        At some point
A biological necessity
Brought such a pressure on the human mind,
This concept floated from it—of a creator
Who made up matter, an imperfect world,
Solely to have an object for his love.

Beautiful and ridiculous. We say:
Love makes the shoots leap from the blunted branches,
Love makes birds call, and maybe we are right.
Love then makes craning saplings crowd for light,
The weak being jostled off to shade and death.
Love makes the cuckoo heave its foster-siblings
Out of the nest, to spatter on the ground.
For love has gouged a temporary hollow
Out of its baby-back, to help it kill.

But who did get it right? Ruth and Naomi,
Tearaway Romeo and Juliet,
Alyosha, Catherine Earnshaw, Jeffrey Dahmer?
They struggled through the thickets as they could.

A wedding entertainment about love
Was set one summer in a wood near Athens.
In paintings by Attila Richard Lukacs,
Cadets and skinheads, city boys, young Spartans
Wait poised like ballet-dancers in the wings
To join the balance of the corps in dances
Passion has planned. They that have power, or seem to,
They that have power to hurt, they are the constructs
Of their own longing, born on the edge of sleep,
Imperfectly understood.

                              Once a young man
Told me my panther made him think of one
His mother's boyfriend had on *his* forearm
—The first man he had sex with, at thirteen.
"Did she know about that?" I asked. He paused:
"I think so. Anyway, they were splitting up."

"Were you confused?"—"No, it was great," he said,
"The best thing that had ever happened to me."

And once, one looked above the wood and saw
A thousand angels making festival,
Each one distinct in brightness and in function,
Which was to choreograph the universe,
Meanwhile performing it. Their work was dance.
Together, wings outstretched, they sang and played
The intellect as powerhouse of love.

> Seems out of place

First Song

David

as on
David &
Goliath

Legend, a drop of dew
cupped in the morning leaf

not true and not untrue
legend before belief
shepherd and youngest son
giantkiller and skald
—am I then anyone—
the roles join, interfold
and firm up as a gist
that moving out of mist
slips with an only tread
into the self ahead

I step with light precision
still ruddy like dawn cloud
the shepherd with the sling
to face a crazy king

joined in the palimpsest
of crisscross gratitude,
and God, and circumcision

Tough with the innocence
you call luck, I the Lord

And though the king has hurled
his javelin at me,

I have his son's love, whence
I learn the mixed demand
I hardly can afford
of jostling with the world

David, and who will he

Incarnate now, and fickle
as the specific tickle
of frenum, fleshy fence
within Bathsheba's hand.

Dancing David

God

my darling and my daily ecstasy

I danced before the Lord, before the Ark,
I whirled and leapt, I danced with all my might,
    Uncovered in the sight
Of slaves and slavegirls, greeting the restored.
My dance was play and yet my play was work
That raised a homage to the appointing Lord.

I tasted sweat even though I wiped it off.
Beyond, I tasted all-approving air
    And cut swathes through it, where
Learning from it an indiscriminate taste
I drew all things to me, however rough,
The harvester in whom God's power is placed.

Saul's daughter watched me through the window-slit,
Despised me, took me for vulgarian,
    A vain and tasteless man.
She said "How glorious was the King today."
Ironic Michal, of the unkind wit,
Taste, taste, good taste will starve your years away.

For finicky taste will pucker up your womb
That shrinks in your disdain before the dance
    Of my uncouth advance,
Until it lose ability to swell,

107

No longer a capacious flexile room
But closed and empty like a light nutshell.

Bathsheba

Much later, in Jerusalem,
While I was walking on my roof
Above my people, watching them,
King, poet, close and yet aloof,

I glimpsed a certain woman nude,
I saw Bathsheba from above
Washing her breasts in solitude,
I learned the imperatives of love.

As for her husband, loyal fighter,
I had a kingly stratagem:
He was to carry me a letter,
All unaware it dealt with him.

I had him posted, for my ends,
In hottest battle of the line
And then abandoned by his friends,
So I could make Bathsheba mine.

Nothing to do, this time, with taste
But with the fervor of the dance
In which I kicked aside, from haste,
Any obstructing circumstance.

A common sequence, I observed:
Love leading to duplicity.

Displeasing to the lord I served,
Also, eventually, to me.

Yet from such commonness and greed
A wiser king than I was grown,
For in our very draining need
The seed of Solomon was sown.

Abishag

All my defiance in the past, I lay
Covered with bedclothes but I gat no heat.

They sought to take the chill off my old age
And found me the lithe virgin Abishag.

She lay on my bosom
                                    oh pubescent girl
Smelling, how lightly, of anxiety,
The source of merely temporary mild heat
So innocent she might have been a dog.

Therefore Bathsheba handsomest of the wives
Entering my room came to the point at once,
Briskly demanding forthwith my assurance
Of the succession for her Solomon,
And took less notice of the girl than if
I had a closed pan of warm embers on me.

I relished secretly what I discovered,
Citron for a parched thought, Abishag
Sweet to the point of sharpness, dense and damp,
A comfort to the memory where I found,
Already present in the God-dance, her—
The ultimate moment of the improvisation,
A brief bow following on the final leap.

Acknowledgements and Notes

Grateful acknowledgements are made to the *Threepenny Review*, where more than a third of these poems first appeared, and also to the following books and periodicals: *A Day Estivall* (ed. Alisoun Gardner-Medwin and Janet Hadley Williams), *A Parcel of Poems*, *After Ovid* (ed. Michael Hofmann and James Lasdun), *Agenda*, *Berkeley Magazine*, *Berkeley Poetry Review*, *Colorado Review*, *Dissent*, *Gulf Coast*, *Hand to Mouth*, *The Independent on Sunday*, *Magma*, *Navis*, *The New Yorker*, *Occident*, *Paris Review*, *PNR*, *Poetry Review*, *Rimbaud Centenary* (Plymouth, 1991), *Salmagundi*, *San Francisco Library Bulletin*, *Slate*, *Sunday Times Books*, *Tikkun*, *Times Literary Supplement*.

"My Mother's Pride" and "The Dump" first appeared as DIA brochures. Some poems appeared in the following pamphlets and limited editions: *Old Stories* (Sea Cliff Press), *Unsought Intimacies* (Peter Koch, illustrated by Theophilus Brown), *In the Twilight Slot* (Enitharmon), *Dancing David* (NADJA, with drawings by Dorothea Tanning), and *Frontiers of Gossip* (Robert L. Barth).

Here are some notes:

(a) on food: in California, a certain kind of sweet-roll is known as a bear-claw; American headcheese is the English brawn; and Total is the brand-name of an American breakfast cereal.

(b) on identities: the American poet Robert Duncan died in 1988; Degen was admired by Thomas Lovell Beddoes; and Jeffrey Dahmer was a serial murderer, cannibal, and necrophile.

(c) miscellaneous: "Arethusa Raped"—Shelley's version, as opposed to Ovid's; "Front Bar of the *Lone Star*"—for the Raphael face, see the Dickensian heroines in the illustrations by Phiz; "Troubadour"—*songs* as in an unwritten opera; but in 1998 all were set to music by Jay Lyon and performed by Len Moors.

And my thanks to Billy Lux.

Printed in the United States
78459LV00002B/37